Wild Chronicles

Did you know!

Lewis Allen

Copyright ©

No part of this book may be reproduced in writing, electronically, by recording, or photocopy without the written permission of the publisher or author.

While every precaution has been taken to verify the accuracy of the information contained herein, the author and publisher accept no responsibility for any errors or omissions. No liability is assumed for damage resulting from the use of the information contained therein.

Table of Contents

Did you know!

Introduction

Dive into the enthralling world of "Wild Chronicles," where each page uncovers a menagerie of astounding animal facts, leading readers on a thrilling safari through the intricate fabric of the animal realm. This engaging investigation, written by Lewis Allen, transcends the everyday, transforming the mundane into a symphony of animal wonders.

Readers will embark on a thrilling trip through untamed settings inhabited by species both alien and familiar in the pages of this beautifully curated compilation. "Wild Chronicles" is a literary ark, transporting readers on a voyage to experience the most exciting and lesser-known sides of the animal universe, from the depths of the ocean's abyss to the soaring heights of mountain peaks.

Imagine diving into the secret societies of the insect world or solving the enigma of migrating birds' amazing navigational abilities. "Wild Chronicles" is more than a book; it's a passport to the wild's hidden storylines, where each fact is a portal into the fascinating lives of our fellow Earthlings.

Join Lewis Allen, your intrepid guide on this zoological adventure, as they uncover the astonishing behaviors, adaptations, and interrelated stories that make the animal kingdom a living tapestry of wonders. Each revelation is a brushstroke in a brilliant painting of life on Earth, from the unfathomable intelligence of octopuses to the symbiotic relationships formed in the heart of jungles.

Prepare to be intrigued, astonished, and enchanted as you read "Wild Chronicles." With Lewis Allen at the helm, this book is more than just a collection of animal statistics; it's a celebration of the diversity, resilience, and sheer brilliance of the creatures who share our world. Step into the wilderness, turn the page, and let "Wild

Chronicles" guide you through the fascinating and awe-inspiring tales of the animal kingdom.

Did you know!

A

Aardvark:

Aardvarks use their lengthy, sticky tongue to eat ants and termites.

To perceive sounds, they have huge, tubular ears that can rotate independently.

Aardvarks are nocturnal species that spend the majority of their time foraging at night.

Albatross:

Albatrosses have enormous wingspanes, with some species reaching 11 feet.

They are very proficient gliders that use ocean winds to go long distances with little effort.

Albatrosses are well-known for their sophisticated courtship rituals, which can include complicated dancing.

Alligator:

Crocodiles have a V-shaped nose, but alligators have a U-shaped snout.

They are outstanding swimmers who can also move fast on land.

Alligators are native to the United States and China and can be found in freshwater settings.

Ant:

Ants exist in colonies, each with its own set of functions, such as workers, soldiers, and a queen.

Some ant species have the ability to carry things up to 50 times their body weight.

Ants are extremely structured and communicate using pheromones.

Anteater:

Anteaters are classified into four species: giant anteater, silky anteater, northern tamandua, and southern tamandua.

Anteaters tear open ant and termite mounds with their powerful claws.

In a single day, the gigantic anteater can ingest up to 30,000 ants and termites.

The Arctic Fox:

Arctic foxes have a thick white fur coat that protects them from the elements in their freezing homes.

They can withstand high temperatures, and their fur changes color with the seasons.

Arctic foxes are omnivores that consume small mammals, birds, and even fruits.

Armadillo:

Armadillos are distinguished by their bony, protective shell, which is made up of overlapping plates.

Armadillos are classified into 20 species, each with its own set of traits.

When threatened, the three-banded armadillo can roll into a ball.

Axolotl:

Axolotls are aquatic salamanders with exceptional regeneration powers.

They have the ability to regrow complete limbs, parts of the heart, and even parts of their brain.

Axolotls are Mexican natives that are critically endangered in the wild.

B

Baboon:

Baboons are African and Arabian sociable primates.

They live in troops, which are hierarchical groups.

Baboons communicate through vocalizations, facial expressions, and grooming.

The Bald Eagle:

The bald eagle is the national bird of the United States and its symbol.

They have a 6 to 7-foot wingspan and are recognized for their strong flying.

Bald eagles are carnivores that frequently hunt fish.

Bat:

Bats are the only mammals that can fly for extended periods of time.

They play an important function in ecosystems by regulating insect populations.

Echolocation is used by some bats to navigate and locate prey.

Beaver:

Beavers are well-known for using sticks and mud to construct dams and lodges.

They have chisel-like teeth that grow continuously throughout their lifetimes.

Beavers are excellent swimmers who can stay underwater for up to 15 minutes.

The Bengal Tiger:

Bengal tigers, which are found in India and Bangladesh, are the most abundant tiger subspecies.

They are great swimmers and frequently cool off in the water.

Bengal tigers live alone and are recognized for their unusual coat patterns.

Bison:

Bison, often known as buffalo, are big animals native to North America and Europe.

They have a big muscle on their back that they utilize to dig through snow.

Bison herds are critical to the preservation of grasslands.

The Blue Jay:

Blue jays are intelligent and noisy birds native to North America.

They are distinguished by their stunning blue, black, and white plumage.

Blue jays are skilled mimics, capable of imitating the sounds of other birds.

The Boa Constrictor is a type of snake.

Non-venomous snakes known as boa constrictors constrict their prey.

They are found in North, Central, and South America's tropical climates.

Because of their flexible jaws, boa constrictors can swallow prey far larger than their heads.

Bonobo:

Bonobos are chimp relatives that live in the jungles of the Democratic Republic of the Congo.

They are well-known for their cooperative and harmonious social structures.

Sexual activity is used by bonobos as a social bonding tool.

Dolphin, Bottlenose:

Bottlenose dolphins are clever marine creatures noted for their playful nature.

In the water, they use echolocation to navigate and hunt for prey.

Bottlenose dolphins live in groups known as pods.

The Brown Bear:

Brown bears can be found in a variety of environments, including forests, mountains, and tundra.

They are omnivores that eat fish, fruit, and small mammals.

During the winter, brown bears hibernate.

Budgerigar:

Budgerigars, sometimes known as budgies, are little Australian parakeets.

They are well-known pets for their ability to mimic human speech.

Budgerigars are gregarious birds that thrive in groups.

Buffalo:

Buffalo are big herbivorous animals native to Africa and Asia.

One of the "Big Five" game animals is the African buffalo.

They are built tough and have characteristic curved horns.

Butterflies:

Butterflies go through metamorphosis as they grow from caterpillars to adults.

Their wings feature specialized scales that produce bright colors and patterns.

Butterflies are important pollinators.

Barracuda:

Barracudas are predatory fish that live in the tropical and subtropical oceans.

They are distinguished by their long, torpedo-shaped bodies and strong fangs.

Barracudas are swift swimmers who hunt in groups.

Binturong:

Binturongs, sometimes known as bear-cats, are Southeast Asian tree-dwelling mammals.

They have a prehensile tail that they utilize to balance and hold branches.

Binturongs have a scent that is comparable to popcorn, earning them the moniker "popcorn bear."

Black Rhinoceros :

African black rhinos are big herbivores with two horns.

They are browsers, eating a wide range of plants and trees.

Poaching for their horns has made black rhinos critically endangered.

Blue Rings octopus:

One of the most venomous marine species is the blue-ringed octopus.

They are small and are frequently seen in tide pools and coral reefs.

Despite their small size, their poison is lethal to humans.

Blue Whale:

Blue whales are the world's largest creatures, with tongues as enormous as elephants.

They are filter feeders, mostly feeding krill, which are tiny shrimp-like organisms.

Blue whales can communicate over long distances by using low-frequency sounds.

C

Cheetah:

Cheetahs are the fastest terrestrial animals, achieving speeds of up to 75 miles per hour in brief bursts.

They have striking black tear stripes on their faces that help to reflect sunlight and improve attention on prey.

Chameleon

Chameleons have the ability to change color in order to blend in with their surroundings and communicate with other chameleons.

Their eyes can move independently, allowing them to see in many directions at the same time.

Chimpanzee:

Chimpanzees are our closest living relatives, sharing approximately 98% of our DNA.

They employ tools for a variety of tasks, such as removing termites from mounds.

Cockatoo:

Cockatoos are intelligent parrots distinguished by their characteristic crests and vocal talents.

They are gregarious birds with strong attachments to their owners.

Crocodile:

Crocodiles are living fossils that have existed for almost 200 million years.

They have strong jaws and are noted for their ambush hunting technique.

Coyote:

Coyotes are versatile canines that can be found all over North America.

They are quite noisy, communicating with a wide range of howls, yips, and barks.

Cub Cheetah:

Cheetah cubs have a characteristic mantle of long fur flowing down their backs, which is considered to discourage predators by mimicking the appearance of honey badgers.

Coral:

Coral reefs, which are constructed by microscopic coral polyps, are home to a wide variety of marine species.

Coral reefs are critical ecosystems that provide habitat, food, and protection to a wide range of marine creatures.

Cow:

Cows have four stomachs, a digestive trait that allows them to break down difficult plant materials efficiently.

Their noses contain a distinct pattern of dots, akin to human fingerprints.

Coyote puppies:

Coyote puppies are born in litters and raised in families.

They are lively and inquisitive, and they are learning important hunting and survival skills from their parents.

Cuttlefish:

Cuttlefish are marine organisms with a distinct internal shell called a cuttlebone that aids in buoyancy control.

For camouflage and communication, they may change the color and texture of their skin.

Caiman:

Caimans are tiny to medium-sized crocodilians that are native to Central and South America.

Caimans, unlike alligators and crocodiles, have bony plates in their skin called osteoderms.

Camel:

Camels have a hump for fat storage and the capacity to cover their nostrils during sandstorms, making them well-adapted to arid conditions.

There are two types of camels: the dromedary, which has one hump, and the Bactrian, which has two humps.

Capuchin Monkey

Capuchin monkeys are highly intelligent and have been observed utilizing tools such as stones to pry open nuts.

They get their name from the prominent cap-like patterns on their heads.

Caracal:

Caracals are medium-sized wild cats distinguished by their tufted ears.

They can catch birds in mid-air and are excellent jumpers.

Centipede:

Centipedes are arthropods with several legs; but, contrary to popular belief, they do not have 100 legs.

They are predators who subdue their prey with venomous claws.

Chinstrap Penguins:

The small black band under their heads gives Chinstrap penguins their name.

They have exceptional swimming abilities and can travel large distances in quest of food.

Chinchilla:

Chinchillas are tiny rodents distinguished by their silky and thick fur.

In their natural high-altitude habitats, they have big ears that aid in heat dissipation.

Clownfish:

Clownfish create symbiotic partnerships with sea anemones, getting protection in exchange for food from the anemones.

They have the ability to change sex, with the dominant individual assuming the female role for reproductive purposes.

Coelacanth:

Coelacanths are prehistoric fish that were considered to be extinct for millions of years until 1938, when a living specimen was discovered.

They are considered "living fossils" and provide important information about the evolution of fish.

Did you know!

D

Dolphin:

Dolphins are extremely intelligent aquatic creatures distinguished by their playful behavior and social systems.

Underwater, they use echolocation to navigate and communicate with one another.

Duck:

Ducks are waterfowl that come in a broad variety of kinds and may be found all over the world.

They have bills designed specifically for separating food from water and dabbling on the surface.

Dachshund:

Dachshunds, often known as wiener dogs, are a tiny breed distinguished by its long body and short legs.

They were bred for hunting but are now popular companion animals.

Dingo:

Dingoes are Australia's natural wild dogs.

They are expert hunters who have adapted to a variety of environments ranging from deserts to woods.

Dormouse:

Dormice are small, nocturnal rodents that hibernate for extended periods of time.

They are arboreal and great climbers.

Dhole:

Dholes are extremely sociable carnivores found in Asia. They are also known as Asiatic wild dogs.

They communicate using a unique whistling mechanism.

Dragonfly:

Dragonflies are insects with huge, multifaceted eyes and powerful flying ability.

They are skilled at hunting smaller flying insects.

The Dung Beetle:

Dung beetles eat excrement and play an important part in nutrient cycling by burying and eating dung.

They navigate by following the Milky Way.

Deer:

Deer are herbivores with antlers that live in a variety of settings around the world.

Bucks, or male deer, grow and lose their antlers on a yearly basis.

Dhole pups:

Dhole pups are born in litters and are collectively cared for by the pack.

Their parents and elder pack members teach them important hunting and social skills.

Dolphin calf:

Dolphin calves are born in the ocean tail-first and must swim to the surface to take their first breath.

They want shelter and advice from their mothers.

Dik-Dik:

Dik-diks are little African antelopes.

They are monogamous and are distinguished by their unusual, prehensile snouts.

Donkey:

Donkeys are horses that have been domesticated.

They are well-known for their intelligence, hard effort, and unusual braying vocalizations.

Duckling:

Ducklings are ducks' young offspring.

They are precocial, which means they are born with their eyes open and ready to move as soon as they hatch.

Dunnart:

Dunnarts are little marsupials that feed insects and are native to Australia.

They are well-known for their speed and ability to leap long distances.

Dabchick:

Dabchicks are little water birds that are also known as little grebes.

They are expert divers who construct floating nests among aquatic plants.

Damselfly:

Damselflies resemble dragonflies but are more delicate in appearance.

They are frequently found around bodies of water and are effective predators of smaller insects.

Desert Tortoise:

Desert tortoises are arid-adapted creatures that can survive for decades.

They can store water in their bladders, helping them to thrive in arid environments.

E

Elephant:

Elephants are the largest land creatures, and they are well-known for their intellect and strong social relationships.

They have lengthy trunks that they use for a variety of purposes such as breathing, grasping items, and communicating.

Eagle:

Eagles are large birds of prey with keen vision and powerful talons.

They are recognized for their spectacular soaring flights and sharp hunting abilities.

The Emperor Penguin

Emperor penguins are the largest penguins and are distinguished by their distinctive black and white plumage.

They live in the Antarctic and are exceptional divers, capable of diving to depths of over 500 meters.

Echidna:

Echidnas are egg-laying monotremes found in Australia and New Guinea.

They have spines on their backs and lengthy, sticky tongues that they use to collect insects.

Elk:

Elk, commonly known as wapiti, are huge herbivores found in North America and Asia with enormous antlers.

During the mating season, the sound of a bugling elk is distinctive and frequently heard.

East African Gorilla:

Eastern gorillas are one of two gorilla species found in the forests of Central and East Africa.

They are herbivores that feed mostly leaves, fruits, and plants.

Eastern Lowlands Gorillas:

Eastern lowland gorillas are the largest of the four subspecies of gorillas.

Because of habitat degradation, hunting, and disease, they are critically endangered.

The Electric Eel:

Electric eels are not actual eels, but rather knifefish with the ability to produce electric shocks.

Electricity is used for navigation, communication, and hunting prey.

Europe Robins:

European robins are tiny birds distinguished by their red breasts.

In European folklore, they are frequently associated with Christmas.

Emu:

Emus are flightless Australian birds.

They are the world's second-largest bird, only being surpassed by the ostrich.

Red Eft (Eft):

The eft is the terrestrial juvenile stage of a salamander called a newt.

Red efts are brilliantly colored, which alerts predators to their toxicity.

Earthworm:

Earthworms are soil-dwelling invertebrates that play a significant role in soil health.

Burrowing through the soil improves aeration and nutrient cycling.

Eagle Ray:

Eagle rays are a type of cartilaginous fish that lives in warm ocean temperatures.

They are recognized for their beautiful swimming and have characteristic, flattened bodies.

Eland:

Elands are Africa's largest antelope species, found in savannas and grasslands.

They are herbivores that eat grasses and leaves.

The Eagle Owl:

Eagle owls are huge owls distinguished by their tufted "ear" feathers.

They hunt at night and have superb vision and hearing.

Edible Frog:

The edible frog is a widespread species in Europe, distinguished by its greenish-brown coloring.

They are frequently seen near ponds and wetlands.

Egyptian Mau:

The Egyptian Mau is a domestic cat breed distinguished by its spotted coat.

They are one of the few breeds that are naturally marked.

Elkhound:

Elkhounds are a breed of northern dog that is well-known for its hunting and herding ability.

One of the most well-known representatives of this breed is the Norwegian Elkhound.

European Salamander:

The European fire salamander is a beautiful amphibian that lives in European woods.

As a protective mechanism, they secrete toxins.

European Shorthair:

The European Shorthair cat breed has a short coat and comes in a range of colors and patterns.

They are well-known for their friendliness

and adaptability.

F

Frozen Frog:

The ability of the wood frog to tolerate frigid temperatures during hibernation is well documented.

It can go into suspended animation and then thaw out when warmer temperatures return.

Finland Spitz:

The Finnish Spitz is a dog breed that is distinguished by its fox-like look and characteristic curled tail.

They were initially raised in Finland to hunt small game.

Fire Salamanders:

Fire salamanders are colorful amphibians with black bodies and yellow markings.

As a protection strategy, they produce toxins from their skin.

Fish Eagle:

Fish eagles, such as the African Fish Eagle, are well-known for their ability to catch fish in the water.

They have a peculiar, haunting call that is frequently heard near watery areas.

Fossa Kits:

Fossa kits, or juvenile fossas, are lively and inquisitive, similar to human kittens.

They practice their hunting abilities by playing in the safety of their family group.

Flatworm:

Flatworms, sometimes known as planarians, are simple invertebrates distinguished by their flattened bodies.

When cut in half, some flatworms can regenerate into two independent individuals.

Flying Lemur:

Flying lemurs, despite their name, are not genuine lemurs and do not fly. They use a patagium to glide.

They are arboreal mammals found in Southeast Asia and are also known as colugos.

Flounder:

Flounders are flatfish with both eyes on the same side of their head.

They are masters of camouflage, seamlessly merging with the seafloor.

Fairy Penguin:

The fairy penguin, commonly known as the little penguin, is the tiniest penguin species.

They are found on the Australian and New Zealand shores.

Fennec Fox Kit:

Kits of the fennec fox are born blind and deaf and rely on their mother for care.

Their huge ears become more apparent as they develop.

Fishing Cat:

Fishing cats are excellent swimmers and are known to hunt fish in wetlands.

They have partially webbed feet and may dive for prey in the water.

Fiddler Rays:

Fiddler rays are cartilaginous fish that have a distinctive violin-shaped pattern on their bodies.

They are frequently discovered on sandy ocean floors.

Fringe- Lipped Bats:

Fringe-lipped bats are so named because their lips are fringed.

They are insectivores that hunt using echolocation.

Fawn of the Fallow Deer:

Fawns of fallow deer are born with markings that help them blend in with their surroundings.

They are self-sufficient and able to stand soon after birth.

Frigatebird Chicks:

Frigatebird chicks are completely reliant on their parents for both food and protection.

They are dependent for a long time before becoming fledglings.

Flamboyant Cuttle:

The colorful and changeable hue of the flamboyant cuttlefish is well known.

It walks on the seafloor with its tentacles and can resemble dangerous flatworms.

Frogmouth:

Frogmouths are nocturnal birds distinguished by their huge, broad mouths and camouflage plumage.

They are skilled hunters who catch insects in flight.

Fruit Bat:

Fruit bats, often known as flying foxes, are important pollinators and seed dispersers.

They have a fox-like visage and are among the world's largest bats.

Fossas Juvenile:

Young fossas, or juveniles, spend a lot of time playing and refining their hunting skills.

They form close bonds with their mothers.

Fur Seal Puppies:

Puppies of fur seals are born on land and rely on their moms for sustenance and protection.

They are distinguished by their thick fur coats.

G

Giraffe:

Giraffes have the world's longest necks, which can reach up to 18 feet.

Their distinctive speckled coat serves as natural camouflage in the African savannah.

Giraffes have the same number of neck vertebrae as humans, despite their long necks.

Gorilla:

Gorillas and humans share approximately 98% of our DNA, making them our closest relatives after chimps.

These primates are herbivores, meaning they eat mostly leaves, stems, and fruits.

Troops of gorillas live in social groups lead by a dominating silverback male.

Gray Wolves:

Gray wolves are extremely gregarious creatures that live and hunt in groups of varying sizes.

They have an advanced communication system that include vocalizations, body language, and scent marking.

Wolves are opportunistic predators that can take down enormous animals like elk and bison.

Great White Shark

The muscular jaws of great white sharks are loaded with serrated teeth.

They are one of the largest predatory fish, reaching lengths of more than 20 feet.

Great white sharks are found in all oceans and are recognized for their speed and agility.

Gecko:

Geckos are well-known for their ability to climb smooth surfaces, owing to unique toe pads that allow them to cling to nearly anything.

Geckos come in over 1,500 different species, each with its own size, color, and habitat.

Geckos are talkative animals that communicate via a variety of vocalizations such as chirps and clicks.

Gazelle:

Because of their remarkable speed and agility, gazelles make challenging prey for predators such as cheetahs.

They are herbivores that mostly graze on grasses and plants.

Gazelles are gregarious creatures that create herds to protect themselves from predators.

Gila Monster:

The Gila monster is a venomous lizard that produces venom in glands in its lower jaw.

The southwestern United States and northwestern Mexico are home to these huge, colorful lizards.

Despite their venom, Gila monsters are slow-moving and pose no serious threat to humans.

Green Sea Turtle

Green sea turtles are distinguished by their distinctive heart-shaped shells and can weigh up to 700 pounds.

They can be found all over the world in tropical and subtropical waters.

Green sea turtles are herbivores that eat sea grasses and algae.

Golden Retriever

Golden retrievers are one of the most popular dog breeds due to their kind and gentle demeanor.

They are extremely clever and are frequently used as guide dogs, therapy dogs, and search and rescue dogs.

Golden retrievers have a waterproof coat and are great swimmers.

Gaur:

The gaur is the largest wild cattle species and is native to South and Southeast Asia.

They have a strong frame with a noticeable hump on their shoulders.

Gaur populations are currently under threat from habitat loss and hunting.

Galapagos Islands Tortoises:

These Galapagos tortoises are noted for their longevity and can live for more than 100 years.

Depending on the island, they have different shell forms and sizes.

The Galapagos tortoises were important in Charles Darwin's theory of evolution.

Gharial:

The gharial crocodile has a long, narrow snout and is critically endangered.

During the breeding season, males have a bulbous protrusion on the tip of their snout that resembles a pot.

They eat fish and live in rivers on the Indian subcontinent.

Glass Frog:

Glass frogs are found in Central and South America and are distinguished by their translucent skin, which allows you to glimpse their internal organs.

They have a vivid green hue on their upper surfaces to help them blend in with the foliage.

Male glass frogs defend and tend to eggs, which distinguishes them from other species.

Gannet:

Gannets are seabirds famous for their spectacular dive diving to hunt fish.

They are distinguished by their brilliant white plumage, black wingtips, and yellowish heads.

On coastal cliffs, gannet colonies can be discovered where they breed and nest.

Genet:

The genet is a small carnivorous mammal that lives in Africa and the Middle East.

They are distinguished by their slim bodies, long tails, and spotted coat patterns.

Genets are adept climbers who are frequently seen in trees.

Ghost Crab:

Ghost crabs are microscopic crabs that can be found on sandy beaches all around the world.

They are named after their pale appearance, which allows them to blend in with sandy settings.

Ghost crabs are nocturnal creatures known for their rapid digging and burrowing abilities.

Anteater Giant:

The gigantic anteater is the largest species of anteater and is native to Central and South America.

They are distinguished by their large snout, prehensile tongue, and bushy tail.

The specialized tongue of giant anteaters allows them to feed on ants and termites.

Glyptodon:

Glyptodons were intriguing creatures that looked like giant, armored armadillos.

They were Pleistocene in age and were distinguished by their huge, domed shells.

Glyptodons were herbivores who most likely used their bony shells to protect themselves.

Goose:

Geese are waterfowl that are distinguished by their characteristic honking cries and V-shaped flight formations.

They are highly migratory and migrate over great areas during the seasons.

Except for Antarctica, every continent has a variety of geese species.

Did you know!

H

Hippopotamus:

After elephants and white rhinos, hippos are the third-largest terrestrial mammals.

Hippos, despite their bulk, are good swimmers and can hold their breath for several minutes.

They release a red, oily material that functions as a natural sunscreen and moisturizer.

Hawk:

Hawks are predatory birds with keen vision and powerful beaks and talons.

They are superb hunters, grabbing prey with pinpoint accuracy while performing mid-air acrobatics.

Red-tailed hawks are one of the most common and easily identified hawk species in North America.

Honeybee:

Honeybees serve an important part in pollination, assisting plants in producing fruits and seeds.

Worker honeybees use sophisticated dancing movements to transmit the location of food sources.

Honeybees make honey by collecting nectar from flowers and converting it through regurgitation and evaporation.

Hedgehog:

Hedgehogs are nocturnal creatures with spines that are modified hairs.

Hedgehogs roll into a tight ball when frightened, protecting themselves with their spines.

They are insectivores, which means they eat insects, small mammals, and plant material.

Hummingbird:

Because of their quick wing beats, hummingbirds are the only birds capable of persistent hovering.

Their hearts may beat up to 1,200 times per minute, and they have a fast metabolism to maintain their high-energy flight.

Hummingbirds are important pollinators because they feed on nectar from flowers.

Harpy Eagle:

Harpy eagles are among the world's largest and most powerful eagles.

They are distinguished by unique feathers on their heads that resemble a crown or "harpy," giving them their name.

Harpy eagles can be found in Central and South America's lush rainforests.

Humpback Whale:

The acrobatic behavior of humpback whales, such as breaching, tail slapping, and singing, is well known.

They are long-distance migrant birds that traverse thousands of miles between feeding and nesting locations.

Humpback whales are well-known for their intricate and melancholy melodies, which are unique to each population.

Hyena:

Hyenas are highly gregarious carnivores with characteristic laughter-like vocalizations.

They have strong jaws and digestive systems that allow them to devour bone and cartilage.

Female hyenas are often larger and more dominating in their social structure than males.

Hammerhead Sharks:

Hammerhead sharks have a distinctive head shape known as a cephalofoil, which improves their sensory awareness.

They are noted for their schooling activity and can be found in both coastal and open ocean regions.

Hammerhead sharks have unique eyes that allow a 360-degree view, which helps them hunt and navigate.

Horned Owl:

Horned owls are nocturnal birds of prey with prominent feathered "horns" on their heads.

They can twist their heads up to 270 degrees to detect prey and have excellent hearing.

Horned owls are adaptive and can be found in a wide range of habitats, including woods and deserts.

Harbor Seal:

Harbor seals are marine mammals that are typically found in Northern Hemisphere shores.

They are distinguished by their "banana-shaped" bodies and are frequently found sunbathing on rocks.

Harbor seals eat a variety of foods, including fish, squid, and crustaceans.

Hummingbird Moth:

The hummingbird moth, despite its name, is an insect, not a bird.

It hovers near flowers, feeding in the manner of a hummingbird.

Because of their similar appearance and flight patterns, hummingbird moths are frequently mistaken for real hummingbirds.

Horseshoe Crabs:

Horseshoe crabs have been alive for around 450 million years and are marine arthropods.

They have blue blood, which is utilized in medicinal applications to identify bacterial contamination.

The pharmaceutical industry relies on horseshoe crabs to test the safety of vaccinations and medical equipment.

Hoatzin:

The hoatzin is a distinctive bird found in the Amazon Rainforest, distinguished by its punk-like crest and blue face.

Hoatzin chicks have claws on their wings, which is unusual among birds and allows them to scale trees.

They are commonly referred to as "stinkbirds" because to the unpleasant stench emitted by their digestive tract.

Howler Monkey:

Howler monkeys have the loudest vocalizations of any land species, with vocalizations that may be heard up to three miles away.

Their prehensile tails enable them to grasp and handle things in the trees.

Howler monkeys are herbivores that eat mostly leaves, fruits, and flowers.

Hagfish:

Hagfish are jawless sea invertebrates renowned for producing slime as a protection strategy.

They have a distinct feeding behavior in which they penetrate the body of larger creatures and consume them from the inside out.

Hagfish are frequently referred to as "living fossils" due to their primitive traits.

Hawk Moth:

Hawk moths are huge, robust insects that fly quickly and agilely.

Some hawk moth species are essential pollinators, particularly in tropical settings.

They are distinguished by their striking resemblance to hummingbirds in both look and behavior.

Hogfish:

Hogfish are brightly colored reef fish that can be found in the Western Atlantic Ocean.

They are well-known for their ability to change color, which aids in camouflage in their coral reef surroundings.

Hogfish root in the sand for small crustaceans and invertebrates with their lengthy snouts.

Hare:

Hares are fast-moving creatures with long hind legs and huge ears.

Hares, unlike rabbits, are born completely furred and with their eyes open.

Hares are accustomed to open-air existence and use their speed and agility to avoid predators.

Hercules Beetle

The Hercules beetle is one of the world's largest beetles, notable for its size and strength.

Male Hercules beetles have big, complex horns on their heads that they use in struggles for territory and mates with rival males.

They are present in tropical rainforests and help with nutrient cycling by breaking down decomposing wood.

Hermit Crab:

Hermit crabs are crustaceans that live in and adopt discarded shells for safety.

They are expert scavengers, consuming a wide range of tiny creatures and organic waste.

Hermit crabs need larger shells as they grow to suit their growing size.

Housefly:

The housefly is a common flying insect that is found all over the world and is generally considered a nuisance.

Houseflies have compound eyes, which allow them to detect movement across a vast area.

They contribute to the ecology by assisting with the breakdown of organic materials.

Hawkfish:

Hawkfish are small, colorful reef fish that are notable for perching on coral fronds.

They are named by their look, which is similar to that of birds of prey due to their flattened bodies and bright colors.

Hawkfish sit on coral branches with their pectoral fins, surveying their environment for prospective prey.

Harlequin Filefish:

The harlequin filefish is a tropical marine fish distinguished by its vivid colors and distinctive body form.

They can change color to blend in with their surroundings, making them useful for camouflage in coral reefs.

The food of harlequin filefish consists of algae and tiny crustaceans.

Harvester (aka Daddy Longlegs):

Harvestmen are arachnids that are commonly referred to as "daddy longlegs."

Harvestmen, unlike spiders, have a fused body structure and no silk glands.

Harvestmen are not poisonous, and their lengthy legs serve a variety of purposes, including sensory perception and predator deterrence.

Hog-nose Snake:

The hog-nosed snake is distinguished by an upturned snout that it employs for burrowing in sandy soil.

When threatened, hog-nosed snakes may roll onto their backs and put out their tongues.

They are nonvenomous and native to North America.

Highland Cow:

Highland cows are a Scottish cattle breed distinguished by their long, shaggy hair and unique curving horns.

They thrive in tough and mountainous locations.

Highland cows are known for their mild demeanor and are frequently shown in attractive settings.

Harbor Porpoise:

The harbor porpoise is one of the smallest cetaceans and can be found in Northern Hemisphere coastal waters.

They are noted for their lively nature, like as riding boat bow waves.

Harbor porpoises eat mostly tiny fish and cephalopods.

Hooded Seal:

The hooded seal gets its name from the inflated, hood-like nasal feature that adult males exhibit during breeding season.

They are accustomed to the chilly Arctic seas and spend the most of their lives at sea.

During the breeding season, hooded seals use vocalizations to communicate with one another.

Hawaiian Monk Seal:

The Hawaiian monk seal is a rare marine mammal that is only found in the Hawaiian Islands.

They have a striking appearance, with a spherical face and skin folds on their neck.

Hawaiian monk seals are threatened by habitat loss, human activity, and disease.

These extra animals beginning with the letter "H" provide a look into the natural world's diversity, stretching from the oceans to the skies and across numerous ecosystems.

Did you know!

Iguana:

Iguanas are huge lizards distinguished by their unique scales and lengthy tails.

They are mostly herbivores that eat leaves, fruits, and flowers.

Some iguanas, such as the marine iguana, can dive for algae and are adept swimmers.

Impala:

Impalas are medium-sized African antelopes.

They are well-known for their capacity to leap up to 10 feet and traverse distances of up to 33 feet.

Impalas have lyre-shaped horns that are only found in males.

Indian Elephant:

Indian elephants are Asia's largest terrestrial mammals.

They are highly clever and gregarious, and they live in small family groups led by a matriarch.

When compared to African elephants, Indian elephants have smaller ears.

Indri:

The indri is a huge live lemur that is native to Madagascar.

They are distinguished by their peculiar wailing calls, which may be heard for considerable distances.

Indris are arboreal creatures that have evolved to living in the treetops.

Ibex:

Ibex are wild goats distinguished by their long, curving horns.

They are well-adapted to steep environments and superb climbers.

Ibex use their horns for defense as well as to maintain authority among their social groups.

Irish Wolfhound

The Irish Wolfhound is a tall dog breed that was originally designed to hunt wolves.

Despite their small stature, they are noted for being peaceful and friendly.

Irish Wolfhounds are known as "gentle giants."

Iriomote Cat:

The Iriomote cat is a wildcat species found only on the Japanese island of Iriomote.

They are critically endangered, with only a small natural population left.

Iriomote cats are superb swimmers that have been observed crossing rivers in quest of prey.

Iguanodon:

Iguanodon is a herbivorous dinosaur genus that lived during the Early Cretaceous period.

They were among the earliest dinosaurs to be identified scientifically.

Iguanodons were distinguished by their thumb spikes and beak-like lips.

Isopod:

Isopods are a crustacean category that includes woodlice and pill bugs.

As a protective tactic, they are noted for rolling into a ball.

Isopods play crucial roles in ecosystems, helping to decompose organic matter.

Ireland Setter:

The Irish Setter is a hunting dog breed distinguished by its exquisite appearance and unique red coat.

They are active, amiable, and frequently succeed in many canine activities.

Irish Setters are used in search and rescue activities due to their excellent sense of scent.

Island Fox:

The island fox is a small fox species found on six of California's eight Channel Islands.

They are the smallest fox species in North America, with adaptations to island living that are unique.

Endangered island fox populations have been successfully conserved through conservation initiatives.

Italian Greyhound:

The Italian Greyhound is a tiny dog breed recognized for its graceful disposition and sleek appearance.

Despite their frail look, they are swift and capable of reaching tremendous speeds.

Italian Greyhounds have a short coat and are popular companion animals.

Irukandji Jellyfish

The Irukandji jellyfish is a small, very venomous jellyfish found in Australian waters.

It is called after the Irukandji people, a community of Indigenous Australians that live in the area.

Despite their diminutive size, their venom can produce Irukandji syndrome, a severe set of symptoms.

Indian Rhinoceros:

The Indian rhinoceros, commonly known as the one-horned rhinoceros, is indigenous to India.

They feature a single horn and skin folds that are thick and armor-like.

Herbivores, Indian rhinoceroses are recognized for their mild demeanor.

Irish Water Spaniel:

The Irish Water Spaniel is one of the oldest and most rare breeds of spaniel.

They have curly, weather-resistant coats and are outstanding water retrievers.

Irish Water Spaniels are distinguished by a prominent "top-knot" of hair on their heads.

Indochina Tiger:

The Indochinese tiger is a tiger subspecies found in Southeast Asia.

They are endangered due to habitat degradation and poaching for body parts.

Indochinese tigers are distinguished by their bright orange coat with dark stripes.

Indian Palm Squirrel:

The Indian palm squirrel, sometimes known as the three-striped palm squirrel, is a tiny rodent found in India.

They are distinguished by their bright fur colors and three dark stripes down their backs.

Indian palm squirrels are quick climbers that live in both urban and rural regions.

Icelandic stallion:

The Icelandic horse is a horse breed that originated in Iceland and is known for its strength, resilience, and distinct gaits.

They have a thick double coat that protects them from harsh weather conditions.

Icelandic horses are well-known for their unique fifth gait, the tölt, which is easy to ride.

Indian Star Tortoise:

The Indian star tortoise is a small to medium-sized tortoise found in South Asia.

They are named after the star-like pattern on their shells.

Indian star tortoises are herbivores that eat on grasses and plants.

Inca Tern:

The Inca tern is a seabird found along South America's shores.

They are distinguished by their white plumage, a mustache-like streak, and red-orange beaks and feet.

Inca terns are adept divers who catch fish with pinpoint accuracy.

Ibiza Wall Lizard:

The Ibiza wall lizard is a lizard species found in the Balearic Islands.

They have a variety of colors, including green, brown, and blue.

Ibiza wall lizards are noted for their ability to survive in both natural and urban areas.

Indian Peafowl (Peacock):

The Indian peafowl, usually known as the peacock, is famed for its spectacular plumage.

Only the males, known as peacocks, have the vivid iridescent feathers.

Peafowls are native to South Asia and are generally linked with beauty and elegance.

Icterine Warbler:

The Icterine warbler is a migratory bird recognized for its lovely song.

They breed in Europe and spend the winter in Africa.

Icterine warblers are commonly found in forests and gardens.

Inchworm (Caterpillar of the Geometer Moth):

Inchworms are the larvae of geometer moths and are distinguished by their looping movement.

They have prolegs on both ends of their bodies, allowing them to securely hold surfaces.

Inchworms are commonly seen as pests in agriculture, although they serve an important role in natural ecosystems.

Iridescent Shark:

A huge freshwater fish native to Southeast Asia, the iridescent shark.

Despite its name, it is a type of catfish, not a shark.

Iridescent sharks are popular in aquariums and can grow to be quite huge.

Ivory-Billed Woodpecker:

The ivory-billed woodpecker is a critically endangered woodpecker species with conflicting sighting reports.

They are distinguished by their black and white plumage and ivory-colored bill.

The ivory-billed woodpecker was originally assumed to be extinct, although it is still considered endangered.

Irish Moiled Cattle:

The Irish Moiled is a rare domestic cow breed unique to Ireland.

Their unique red or dun coat and white markings set them apart.

Irish Moiled cattle are noted for their ability to adapt to a variety of situations.

Indian Scorpion:

The Indian red scorpion is a deadly arachnid that can be found throughout India.

It is one of the most dangerous scorpions, and its sting can be fatal.

Indian red scorpions are nocturnal and are frequently seen in and around human-made structures.

These new animals beginning with the letter "I" add to the wide and intriguing

Did you know!

world of fauna, which includes everything from birds and reptiles to insects and mammals.

J

Jaguar:

Jaguars are the world's third-largest big cat species, behind tigers and lions.

They have a powerful bite and are noted for their ability to pierce their prey's skulls or shells.

Jellyfish:

Jellyfish have been present for about 500 million years, making them one of the oldest animal groupings still alive.

While jellyfish are commonly thought to be simple organisms, some demonstrate complicated activities such as coordinated swimming.

Jackal:

Jackals are opportunistic omnivores with a diverse diet that includes small mammals, birds, insects, and fruits.

They are noted for their social tendencies, frequently living in family groupings and hunting together.

Jay:

Jays are very intelligent birds with the ability to replicate sounds, including human speech.

They play an important part in forest ecosystems by aiding in seed dispersal.

Jaguarundi:

Jaguarundis are one of the only cat species capable of a wide range of vocalizations, including chirps, whistles, and even purrs.

Jaguarundis, unlike many other wild cats, are mostly diurnal, meaning they are active during the day.

Japanese Chin:

The Japanese Chin is well-known for its cat-like grooming, frequently wiping its face with its front paws.

Because it was frequently preserved by Japanese nobles and aristocracy, this breed has a regal history.

Javan Rhino:

Javan rhinos are the most endangered rhino species, with only a small population living in Java, Indonesia's Ujung Kulon National Park.

Females are significantly larger than males and have a single horn.

Jerboa:

Jerboas are desert-adapted, with modified kidneys that allow them to collect water from their meal.

Jerboas can leap many feet into the air and cover long distances with each jump thanks to their muscular hind legs.

These intriguing facts demonstrate the range of features and behaviors among animals beginning with the letter "J." Each species has its own unique adaptations that let it survive and play an ecological role.

K

Kangaroo:

Kangaroos are marsupials famed for their muscular rear legs that allow them to hop.

Female kangaroos have a pouch in which they carry and nurse their young, known as joeys.

Koala:

Koalas are arboreal marsupials native to Australia that are often referred to as "koala bears," despite the fact that they are not bears.

They are particularly discriminating eaters due to their specific diet of eucalyptus leaves.

Kingfisher:

Kingfishers are brightly colored birds with long, unique bills and superb fishing abilities.

They are frequently spotted perched near bodies of water, preparing to plunge in and catch fish.

Komodo Dragon:

The Komodo dragon is the largest lizard species found in Indonesia.

They have an acute sense of smell and are notorious for their poisonous bite.

Orca (Killer Whale):

Killer whales, often known as orcas, are extremely intelligent marine creatures with sophisticated social structures and communication abilities.

They are apex predators with a varied diet that includes fish, seals, and even other whales.

Kookaburra:

Kookaburras are huge, terrestrial kingfishers that are indigenous to Australia and New Guinea.

Their call sounds like laughter, earning them the moniker "laughing kookaburra."

Kudu:

Kudus are big African antelopes notable for their spiral horns.

Male kudus have larger, more twisted horns than females.

Kangaroo Rat:

Kangaroo rats are rodents that live throughout North America, primarily in desert areas.

They are adapted to arid settings and can go without water, relying on moisture from their diet.

Koel:

The koel is a cuckoo bird native to Asia and Australia.

In certain civilizations, the koel's characteristic call heralds the arrival of the monsoon season.

Kestrel:

Kestrels are little falcons recognized for their superb hunting abilities and hovering flight.

They have acute vision and can sense ultraviolet light, which helps them locate prey.

Koi Carp:

Koi fish are decorative variations of common carp that are commonly kept in ponds because of their brilliant colors.

Koi are connected with perseverance, fortitude, and good fortune in Japanese culture.

Kiwi:

Kiwis are flightless birds native to New Zealand that are distinguished by their small size, long beaks, and unusual look.

Among all bird species, they deposit the largest eggs in comparison to their body size.

King Cobra:

The world's longest venomous snake, the king cobra, is found throughout South and Southeast Asia.

It is not a real cobra, despite its name, and belongs to a different genus.

Kangal the Dog:

The Kangal is a livestock guardian dog breed from Turkey that is recognized for its power, devotion, and protective instincts.

It is frequently used to protect livestock from predators, particularly sheep.

Kakapo:

The kakapo, often known as the night parrot, is a severely endangered nocturnal parrot indigenous to New Zealand.

It is noted for its friendliness and curiosity, yet it is under threat from invasive predators.

These intriguing facts reveal the different and distinct qualities of animals whose names begin with the letter "K." Each species plays an important part in its ecosystem and contributes to the beauty and complexity of the natural world.

L

Lion:

Lions are the only social large cats that live in groups known as prides.

Male lions are easily identified by their magnificent manes.

Leopard:

Leopards are adept climbers and frequently store their kills in trees to keep scavengers at bay.

Their fur has a characteristic rosette pattern.

Lynx:

Lynxes have tufted ears that allow them to hunt in snowy conditions.

The Canada lynx is distinguished by its long legs and big, well-furred feet that function as snowshoes.

Llama:

Llamas are domesticated South American camel that are used to transport loads in steep areas.

They are noted for being gentle and can make excellent therapy animals.

Lemur:

Lemurs are primates that can only be found on the island of Madagascar.

They are distinguished by their huge, reflecting eyes and unusual vocalizations.

Lynx Spiders:

Lynx spiders are well-known for their keen vision and hunting abilities.

They are named because the tufts of fur on their legs and their cat-like motions.

Lizard:

Lizards are a diverse group of reptiles that come in a variety of sizes and characteristics.

Some lizards have the ability to regenerate lost tails as a protection strategy against predators.

Ladybug:

Ladybugs, often known as ladybirds, are beneficial insects that consume aphids and other pests.

Their striking hues alert predators to the fact that they taste awful.

Lobster:

Lobsters are crustaceans that live in the waters and are known for having powerful claws.

They communicate by combining touch and chemical messages.

Lynx Catfish:

Lynx catfish are freshwater fish with long, filamentous pectoral fins that resemble the ears of a lynx.

They are well-known in the aquarium sector for their placid temperament.

Limpet:

Limpets are conical-shelled marine gastropod mollusks.

They have a powerful muscular foot that allows them to cling to rocks tightly.

Liger:

A liger is an offspring of a male lion and a female tiger.

Ligers are among the largest big cats, with characteristics inherited from both parent species.

Labrador Retriever:

Labrador Retrievers are a popular dog breed recognized for their friendliness and intelligence.

Guide dogs, search and rescue dogs, and therapy dogs are all common uses for them.

The Leafcutter Ant:

Leafcutter ants are noted for bringing leaves back to their nests to produce fungus for food.

They have extremely structured and complicated social structures.

Lynx Monkey:

The lynx monkey, often known as the brown capuchin, is a South American New World monkey.

They are recognized for their cleverness and use of tools, such as extracting insects from tree bark using sticks.

These facts provide a look into the range of creatures whose names begin with the letter "L." From stately large cats to hardworking insects and adored domesticated pets, each species adds to the colorful fabric of the animal kingdom.

Did you know!

M

Monkey:

Monkeys are intelligent primates recognized for having opposable thumbs.

Capuchin monkeys have been observed extracting insects from tree bark using tools such as sticks.

Moose:

Moose are the largest members of the deer family, distinguished by their palmate antlers.

They are strong swimmers who can cross enormous bodies of water.

Mantis Shrimp:

Mantis shrimps hunt with their extraordinarily swift and powerful claws.

Their eyes are among the most advanced in the animal kingdom, with the ability to see polarized light and a wider range of hues than humans.

Meerkat:

Meerkats are small carnivorous mammals that live in social groups known as mobs or clans.

They are notable for standing upright on their hind legs and balancing on their tails.

Manatee:

Manatees are big herbivorous marine mammals that are also known as sea cows.

They are delicate creatures that prefer warm coastal waters.

Magpie:

Magpies have black and white plumage and are highly intelligent birds.

They have been observed imitating human speech and other sounds.

Mongoose:

Mongooses are little carnivores that are well-known for their agility and ability to kill venomous snakes.

Some mongoose species live in social groups, while others are solitary.

Millipede:

Millipedes are arthropods with several legs, albeit they do not have a thousand.

They are notable for their cylindrical bodies and play a vital role as detritivores in ecosystems.

Macaw:

Macaws are huge, brightly colored parrots that are native to Central and South America.

They are distinguished by their colorful plumage and strong, bent beaks.

Mountain Goat:

Mountain goats are hoofed mammals that have evolved to life in mountainous areas.

They are skilled climbers who are frequently spotted mounting steep cliffs.

Monitor Lizard:

Monitor lizards are enormous reptiles that are distinguished by their long bodies, muscular tails, and razor-sharp claws.

The largest lizard species is the Komodo dragon, a type of monitor lizard.

Moles:

Moles are small burrowing mammals with dig-specific front limbs.

They have silky fur that allows them to travel through tunnels with ease.

Maned Wolf:

The maned wolf is a huge canid with lengthy legs and a fur-covered mane around its neck.

It is not related to wolves, despite its name, and is a distinct species.

Manta Rays:

Manta rays are enormous, filter-feeding rays that can be found in tropical waters.

They feature horn-like cephalic fins that assist guide plankton-rich water into their mouths.

Marmoset:

Marmosets are little primates with claw-like nails and specialized teeth for scraping tree bark for gum.

Exotic pets frequently include common marmosets.

These facts offer a look into the vast world of animals whose names begin with the letter "M." From primates to marine mammals, insects to reptiles, each species adds to Earth's unique tapestry of life.

Did you know!

N

Narwhal:

Narwhals are toothed whales notable for their long, spiral tusks that can grow to be 10 feet (3 meters) long.

The tusk is an extended tooth that is utilized for communication as well as breaking through sea ice.

Nightingale:

Nightingales are small, extremely vocal birds recognized for their elaborate and exquisite songs.

Their strong and melodic singing is frequently connected with the coming of spring.

Newt:

Newts are amphibians with colorful skin and the ability to repair lost body parts.

They have a long life cycle that includes an aquatic larval stage and a terrestrial adult stage.

Nudibranch:

Nudibranchs are brightly colored sea slugs that come in a wide range of shapes and sizes.

They are distinguished by their vivid colors, which act as a signal to predators that they are toxic.

Numbat:

Numbats are termite-eating marsupials native to Australia.

They are also known as banded anteaters because of their striking striped coat.

Nile Crocodile:

Nile crocodiles are one of the largest crocodile species, inhabiting watery habitats in Sub-Saharan Africa.

They are formidable predators noted for their stealth and ambush hunting tactics.

Nuthatch:

Nuthatches are little birds that can fly headfirst down tree trunks.

They are well-known for burying nuts and seeds in bark cracks and then "hatching" them open with their bills.

Numbray:

Numbrays, sometimes known as numbfishes, are electric rays that live in coastal waters.

To protect themselves and locate prey, they may generate electric shocks.

Norsefish:

Norsefish, sometimes known as hake, are cold-water deep-sea fish.

They have a lengthy body and play a significant role in commercial fishing.

Nalolo:

The nalolo, also known as the Napoleon wrasse, is a huge coral reef fish native to the Indo-Pacific.

It is distinguished by a pronounced hump on the brow and brilliant colors.

Nandu:

Nandu, sometimes known as rheas, are flightless South American birds.

They are the continent's largest bird species and relatives of the ostrich and emu.

Nematode:

Nematodes, sometimes known as roundworms, are a varied genus of worms that live in a variety of settings.

Some nematodes are parasites, whereas others perform important roles in soil nutrient cycle.

Numbfish:

Numbfish, often known as electric rays, are cartilaginous fish that can deliver electric shocks.

They live in coastal seas and use their electric skills to defend themselves and navigate.

Nase:

The Nase is a freshwater fish found in European rivers.

They are members of the Cyprinidae family and are distinguished by their unique downturned jaws.

These facts showcase the variety of animals whose names begin with the letter "N," highlighting species from various habitats and ecosystems.

Did you know!

O

Ocelot:

Ocelots are wild cats found in the Americas that are distinguished by their lovely spotted coats.

They are excellent climbers and swimmers, and their name comes from the Aztec word "tlalocelot," which means "field tiger."

Ostrich:

Ostriches are the world's largest and heaviest birds.

They lack flight but are great runners with long, powerful legs.

Orangutan:

Orangutans are large apes found in Borneo and Sumatra jungles.

They are extremely intelligent and share approximately 97% of their DNA with humans.

Octopus:

Octopuses are highly intelligent marine animals capable of intricate problem solving.

They have three hearts and can hide by changing the color and texture of their skin.

The Ocelot Catfish:

Ocelot catfish are freshwater fish with eye-catching spotted markings.

They are native to South America and are popular in the aquarium trade.

Otter:

Otters are semi-aquatic mammals known for their antics.

They crack up shellfish with instruments such as pebbles.

Owl:

Owls are prey birds distinguished by their peculiar sounds and silent flight.

They have unique feathers that let them fly quietly.

Olive Baboons:

Olive baboons are monkeys native to Africa.

They dwell in big social groups known as armies and have sophisticated social structures.

Oropendola:

Oropendolas are migratory birds that live throughout Central and South America.

They are famed for their powerful and melodious calls and for building unusual hanging nests.

Oxpecker:

Oxpeckers are birds that coexist with huge mammals such as buffalo and rhinoceroses.

They prey on ticks and parasites found on the skin of mammals.

Oyster:

Oysters are bivalve mollusks that live in both salt and fresh water.

By purifying water, they play an important role in marine ecosystems.

Okapi:

Okapis are giraffe relatives that live in Central African jungles.

Their legs are striped like zebras, and they have a large, prehensile tongue.

Oriole:

Orioles are brightly colored migratory birds recognized for their unusual melodies.

They frequently construct tree-hanging nests.

Onager:

The onager is a wild Asian donkey native to Iran's deserts.

They are well-known for their endurance and speed.

Ostracod:

Ostracods are microscopic crustaceans that are usually referred to as seed shrimp.

They can be found in a variety of aquatic environments, including freshwater and marine environments.

These facts provide a glimpse into the fascinating world of animals whose names begin with the letter "O," highlighting a variety of species from various habitats and regions.

Did you know!

P

Penguin:

Penguins are flightless birds, yet they are great swimmers.

The Emperor Penguin is the largest penguin species, with the ability to dive to depths of 1,800 feet (550 meters).

Penguins frequently create vast colonies to breed and protect themselves.

Panda:

Giant Pandas are endemic to China and are distinguished by their striking black and white fur.

Pandas primarily consume bamboo, but they are carnivores.

Despite their stature, pandas are adept tree climbers.

Parrot:

Parrots are well-known for their bright plumage and ability to mimic human speech.

The intelligent and curious Kea parrot is indigenous to New Zealand.

Parrots have zygodactyl feet, which have two forward and two backward toes.

Pangolin:

Pangolins are a type of animal with thick, overlapping keratin scales.

Pangolins are found in Africa and Asia, and there are eight different species.

Pangolins are the only animals with scales, and when frightened, they curl up into a ball.

Peacock:

The male peafowl is known as a peacock, while the female is known as a peahen.

Peafowls are recognized for their lavish and colorful plumage, particularly the male's stunning tail feathers.

Microscopic crystal-like structures cause the iridescent colors on a peacock's feathers.

Platypus:

The platypus is an Australian mammal notable for its duck-bill, webbed feet, and egg laying.

Platypuses can stay submerged for several minutes and are superb swimmers.

The hind legs of male platypuses bear venomous spurs.

Porcupine:

Porcupines are rodents with sharp quills that they employ for protection.

Contrary to popular opinion, porcupines cannot shoot their quills; rather, the quills include barbs that make removal difficult.

Porcupines are classified into two types: Old World porcupines and New World porcupines.

Puma:

Pumas, sometimes known as cougars or mountain lions, are huge cats native to the Americas.

Pumas are noted for their solitary nature and are exceptional jumpers and climbers.

They have a diverse vocal repertoire that includes screams, growls, and purrs.

Python:

Pythons are constrictor snakes found all over the world.

The reticulated python is the world's longest snake, reaching lengths of more than 20 feet (6 meters).

Pythons are non-venomous and use constriction to kill their prey.

Puffin:

Puffins are seabirds with distinctively colored beaks, particularly during the breeding season.

They are adept fliers and swimmers who "fly" underwater in quest of fish using their wings.

Puffin colonies are frequently found on cliffs and rocky islands.

Praying Mantis:

Praying mantises are predatory insects distinguished by their peculiar stance, which mimics that of a praying mantis.

They are adept hunters who can capture and consume insects much larger than themselves.

Female praying mantises are known to consume male praying mantises after mating.

Proboscis Monkeys:

Proboscis monkeys are distinguished by their long, bulbous noses, which are especially prominent in males.

They are superb swimmers and have been observed leaping into rivers to avoid predators.

Proboscis monkeys live largely along the coasts of Borneo and Sumatra.

Prairie Canine:

Prairie dogs are little burrowing rodents that thrive in vast colonies in North American prairies.

They are very gregarious animals with a complicated communication system of barks and chirps.

Prairie dogs, despite their name, are not dogs but are named for their barking cries.

Ptarmigan:

Ptarmigans are birds that thrive in cold, alpine habitats.

For camouflage, they change the color of their plumage to white in the winter and brown in the summer.

Ptarmigans can be found in North America, Europe, and Asia's Arctic and subarctic regions.

Prawn:

Prawns are crustaceans that are related to shrimp but larger and with a somewhat different body structure.

They are a key part of marine ecosystems and a popular source of seafood.

Prawns come in a variety of colors, and their look varies depending on the species.

Prairie Rattlesnake:

The prairie rattlesnake is a venomous snake native to North America with a unique rattling tail.

They are critical in managing rodent populations in their natural settings.

Prairie rattlesnakes are generally shy and will often try to avoid human contact.

Peacock Spider:

Peacock spiders are little jumping spiders with brightly colored abdomen markings.

Male peacock spiders engage in complex courtship displays that include sophisticated leg movements and abdomen lifting.

Peacock spiders are widespread in Australia, and each species has its own courtship dance.

The Painted Turtle:

Painted turtles are North American freshwater turtles.

Their colorful markings on their shells give them their name.

Painted turtles are known to sunbathe on rocks or logs.

Peregrine Falcon:

The peregrine falcon is a strong bird of prey recognized for its amazing speed and agility.

They are among the fastest creatures, with dives reaching speeds of nearly 240 mph (386 km/h).

Except for Antarctica, peregrine falcons can be found on every continent.

Pika:

Pikas are little mountain mammals that are related to rabbits.

They are recognized for their unique vocalizations and are frequently referred to as "whistling hares."

Pikas are cold-adapted and do not hibernate throughout the winter.

Peafowl:

Peafowl are huge, colorful birds with elaborate plumage.

The male is known as a peacock, and the female is known as a peahen.

Peafowls are indigenous to South Asia but have spread to many other regions of the world.

Porcupine fish:

Porcupine fish are marine fish notable for their ability to inflate their bodies into a spiky ball when threatened.

They feature razor-sharp spines that keep predators at bay.

Porcupine fish live in tropical and subtropical waters.

Peacock Mantis Shrimps:

Mantis shrimps, especially the peacock mantis shrimp, are saltwater crustaceans distinguished by their vibrant colors and powerful hunting ability.

They have advanced eyes that can perceive polarized light and utilize powerful "clubs" to attack victims.

Coral reefs are home to the peacock mantis shrimp.

Potoo:

Potoos are nocturnal birds that are native to Central and South America.

They have huge eyes and a broad, gaping mouth, giving them a striking appearance.

Potoos are recognized for their remarkable camouflage, which allows them to seem like tree branches during the day.

Pocket Gophers:

Pocket gophers are burrowing rodents with fur-lined cheek pouches that they use to transport food.

They are important in soil turnover and plant dissemination.

Pocket gophers can be found in North and Central America.

Did you know!

Q

Quokka:

The quokka is a small herbivorous mammal endemic to Australia that has a pleasant and smiling demeanor.

They are frequently described to as the "happiest animal in the world" because of their presumably happy facial expressions.

Quokkas are herbivores that eat mostly grasses and leaves.

Quetzal:

The dazzling quetzal is a brightly colorful bird found in Central America, particularly in Mexico and Central America's cloud forests.

It is Guatemala's national bird and is recognized for its gorgeous iridescent green and red plumage.

Quetzals have long tail feathers and are culturally significant to the region's indigenous inhabitants.

Quail:

Quails are small to medium-sized birds that can be found in a wide range of settings around the world.

They are ground-dwelling birds distinguished by their characteristic "bobwhite" sounds.

Quails are frequently shot for sport as well as for their eggs, which are considered a delicacy in some cultures.

Queen Alexandra Birdwing Butterfly :

The Queen Alexandra's birdwing is the world's largest butterfly, native to Papua New Guinea.

These butterflies, named after Queen Alexandra of England, have a wingspan of up to a foot (30 cm).

They are distinguished by their vibrant colors and unique wing designs.

Quahog:

The quahog is a type of hard-shelled clam found in North American coastal waters.

Native American cultures have been eating quahogs for years, and they are also known for producing pearls, but they are usually not as precious as those from oysters.

In the northeastern United States, the phrase "quahog" is widely used to refer to the clam.

While the list of animals beginning with "Q" is short, these creatures exhibit a wide range of qualities, from the quetzal's distinctive and bright appearance to the quokka's endearing demeanor.

Did you know!

R

Raccoon:

Raccoons are versatile mammals distinguished by their characteristic facial features and ringed tails.

They are omnivores who wash their food in water before eating it.

Red Panda:

Red pandas are tiny, tree-dwelling mammals that are indigenous to the eastern Himalayas and southwestern China.

Red pandas, despite their name, are not related to gigantic pandas. They belong to the Ailuridae family.

Reindeer:

Reindeer, commonly known as caribou in North America, are huge herbivorous mammals that live in the arctic and subarctic regions.

They are well-known for their seasonal migrations and have cultural significance in many indigenous communities.

Rhinoceros:

Rhinoceroses are huge herbivores with horns on their snouts and thick skin.

Rhinos are found in Africa and Asia in five different kinds.

Rhinos are critically threatened owing to horn poaching.

Ring-tailed lemur

Ring-tailed lemurs are Madagascar-native primates with long, banded tails and striking facial features.

They are extremely gregarious and live in groups known as soldiers.

River Otter:

River otters are aquatic mammals that live in rivers, lakes, and along the coast.

They are noted for their playful activity, which includes tumbling down riverbanks and snow-covered hills.

Roadrunner:

Roadrunners are little birds that live on the ground in North and Central America.

They are distinguished by their unusual look, long tail, and fast running ability.

The greater roadrunner is New Mexico's state bird.

Rock hopper Penguins:

Rock hopper penguins are crested penguins distinguished by their characteristic hopping movements over rocky ground.

They live on sub-Antarctic islands.

Rottweiler:

The Rottweiler is a large domestic dog breed recognized for its power, loyalty, and striking black and tan coat.

They were developed as herding dogs before becoming famous as guard dogs.

Russian Blue Cat:

The Russian Blue cat breed is distinguished by its exquisite appearance, short dense hair, and eye-catching green eyes.

They are known for being shy in the presence of outsiders yet building deep ties with their owners.

S

Sloth:

Sloths are slow-moving creatures that are native to Central and South America.

They spend the majority of their time upside down in trees.

Because sloths have a slow metabolism and move slowly, algae can grow on their fur.

Snow Leopard:

Snow leopards are huge cats native to Central and South Asian mountain ranges.

They are well-adapted to live in cold, high-altitude situations due to their attractive spotted coat.

Snow leopards are considered vulnerable owing to habitat loss and poaching.

Sea turtle:

Sea turtles are marine reptiles that live in waters all around the world.

They are distinguished by their unusual shells and can travel hundreds of miles between nesting and feeding locations.

Pollution, habitat loss, and climate change pose risks to various sea turtle species, including the loggerhead and leatherback.

Shark:

Sharks are a group of fish that have cartilaginous bones.

They've been around for about 400 million years, which makes them older than dinosaurs.

Sharks are found in about 500 different species, ranging from the tiny dwarf lanternshark to the huge whale shark.

Spider:

Spiders are arachnids with eight legs and the ability to spin silk.

They play an important role in insect population management by trapping them in webs.

Some spiders, such as the wolf spider, actively hunt their prey rather than weave webs.

Sea Star (starfish):

Starfish are radially symmetrical sea creatures with tube feet.

They can restore lost arms, and some species may regenerate an entire new body from a single arm and a portion of the central disk.

Starfish, despite their name, are not fish.

Siberian Tiger:

The Siberian tiger, sometimes known as the Amur tiger, is the world's largest big cat, native to eastern Russia, China, and North Korea.

They have a thick coat to keep warm and are recognized for their strength and agility.

Siberian tigers are threatened by habitat loss and poaching.

Sparrow:

Sparrows are tiny, brown and gray passerine birds found all over the world.

They are well-known for their ability to adapt to urban situations and are frequently found in cities.

Sparrows are gregarious birds that frequently move in groups.

Sperm Whale:

Sperm whales are the largest toothed whales, with huge skulls and protruding foreheads.

They have the world's largest brain of any mammal.

Sperm whales are deep-diving oceanic creatures that eat enormous squid.

Serval:

The serval is an African wild cat with a slim body, long legs, and huge ears.

They are exceptional jumpers and can catch birds in mid-air.

Servals can be found in a range of settings, including savannas and woods.

Stingray:

Stingrays have flat bodies and long, whip-like tails.

They are frequently seen in tropical and subtropical coastal waters.

For self-defense, certain stingray species contain venomous barbs on their tails.

Sable Antelope:

Sable antelopes are huge, dark-colored antelopes that are indigenous to southern Africa.

Males have long, curving horns that can grow to be 1.5 meters long.

They have a distinctive appearance and are commonly seen in grasslands and savannas.

Sand Dollar:

Sand dollars are water creatures that are linked to sea urchins and starfish.

They have a flattened, disk-like shape and are frequently discovered on sandy ocean beds.

Sand dollars have a remarkable five-fold symmetry pattern on their tests (skeletons).

Salmon:

Salmon are migratory fish that can be found in both freshwater and saltwater.

They are famous for their extraordinary ability to swim upstream to spawn.

Salmon are an important aspect of aquatic ecosystems and an important economic resource in the fishing industry.

Siamang:

Siamangs are big, black-furred gibbons native to Southeast Asia's forests.

They are distinguished by a unique neck pouch that amplifies their sounds.

Siamangs are primarily arboreal, spending the majority of their lives in trees.

Sawfish:

Sawfish are huge rays with a saw-like long, flattened rostrum (snout).

They inhabit warm coastal waters and estuaries.

Sawfish are critically endangered due to habitat loss and exploitation and are noted for their distinct appearance.

Sloth Bear:

Sloth bears are native to the Indian subcontinent and are distinguished by their shaggy fur and unusually pointed snouts.

They are adept climbers and frequently feed on insects, particularly termites.

Due to habitat degradation and poaching, sloth bears are classed as vulnerable.

Sandhill Crane:

Sandhill cranes are migratory birds native to North America.

They are distinguished by their peculiar bugling sounds and spectacular courtship rituals.

Sandhill cranes fly in V-shaped formations on extended journeys.

Sablefish:

Sablefish, sometimes known as black cod, are North Pacific deep-sea fish.

Because of their high oil content, their meat is delicate and tasty.

Sablefish have a high commercial value in the fishing sector.

Scorpion:

Scorpions are arachnids that are distinguished by their pincers and a segmented tail that may include a poisonous stinger.

Except for Antarctica, they can be found on every continent.

While some scorpions have strong venom, the vast majority are not deadly to humans.

These animals demonstrate the broad spectrum of living forms that begin with the letter "S." The natural world is replete with fascinating creatures, from the depths of the ocean to the treetops of the rainforest.

Did you know!

T

Tiger:

Tigers are the world's largest cats, distinguished by their unique orange coat with black stripes.

They are strong predators that can take down animals much larger than themselves.

Tigers are a critically endangered animal, with several subspecies facing major conservation concerns.

Turtle:

Turtles are reptiles with protective shells that live in a variety of ecosystems, including marine and freshwater habitats.

Some turtles, such as the leatherback sea turtle, have extended migrations.

Turtles have existed for millions of years, evolving during the dinosaur era.

Toucan:

Toucans are brilliantly colored birds found in Central and South America with big, unique bills.

Their bills are light and essentially hollow, but they are remarkably powerful.

Toucans are frugivorous, meaning they eat mostly fruits but sometimes insects and small mammals.

Tarantula:

Tarantulas are big, hairy spiders found all over the world.

Most tarantulas are not dangerous to people, despite their frightening look.

They use silk to build burrows or webs for protection.

Tapir:

Tapirs are big herbivorous mammals with an unusually long snout.

They are good swimmers and frequently live near bodies of water.

Tapirs can be found in Central America, South America, and Southeast Asia.

Tortoise:

Tortoises are reptiles that live on land and have a thick, domed shell.

They are well-known for their longevity, with some species lasting for well over a century.

Tortoises are herbivores that eat grasses and other vegetation.

Tarsier:

Tarsiers are small monkeys native to Southeast Asia, distinguished for their big eyes and nocturnal activity.

They have the largest eyes in comparison to their body size of any mammal.

Tarsiers are expert hunters who catch insects and tiny vertebrates.

Thresher Shark:

Thresher sharks are distinguished by their long tails, which they utilize to shock victims.

They can be found all around the world in temperate and tropical waters.

Thresher sharks are well-known for their exceptional leaping abilities.

Tiger Shark:

Tiger sharks are huge predatory sharks with dark striped bodies.

They are known for their scavenging activity and can be found in tropical and temperate oceans.

Tiger sharks have a diverse diet and are frequently referred to as the "garbage cans of the sea."

Tamarin:

Tamarins are small, fast-moving monkeys native to Central and South America.

They are noted for their gregarious behavior and frequently reside in families.

Tamarins use a variety of vocalizations and body language to communicate.

These are just a few examples of animals that begin with the letter "T." Each of these species has distinct qualities that contribute to Earth's remarkable diversity of life.

Turkey:

Turkeys are huge North American birds.

Wild turkeys have the ability to fly and are extremely adaptive, but domesticated turkeys are kept for meat.

Male turkeys are referred to as toms or gobblers, while females are referred to as hens.

Tiger Beetle:

Tiger beetles are predatory insects with lightning-fast sprinting speeds.

They are found in a variety of locations around the world, and some species are brilliantly colored.

Tiger beetles are fast predators who use their speed to get their prey.

Tuatara:

The tuatara is a New Zealand native reptile that is often referred to as a living fossil.

Although it looks like a lizard, the tuatara has certain distinguishing features, including a third eye on top of its head.

Tuataras have a slow metabolism and a lengthy lifespan, with some living for more than a century.

Tayra:

Tayras are weasel-like mammals native to Central and South America.

They are nimble climbers with a keen sense of curiosity and intellect.

Tayras eat a variety of foods, including fruits, insects, and small mammals.

Tuna:

Tunas are huge, fast-swimming fish that can be found in warm oceans all around the world.

They are significant in commercial fishing and are distinguished by their streamlined bodies.

Some tuna species, such as the bluefin tuna, migrate extensively.

Tortoiseshell Buttreflies:

Tortoiseshell butterflies are a type of colorful butterfly with eye-catching designs.

They can be found all across the planet and frequently move large distances.

The painted lady butterfly is a well-known species of tortoiseshell butterfly.

Tentacled Snake:

Tentacled snakes are non-venomous aquatic snakes native to Southeast Asia.

It has tentacles on its snout that sense movement in the water.

Tentacled snakes have evolved to thrive in watery habitats.

Toucan Toco:

Toco toucans are the largest toucan species, distinguished by their wide, colorful bills.

They are indigenous to South America and play an important role in seed dissemination.

Toco toucans have distinctive vocalizations, including a croaking call.

Trapdoor Spider:

Burrowing spiders with a silk-lined burrow with a hinged lid are known as trapdoor spiders.

They use their burrows to ambush any approaching prey.

Trapdoor spiders can be found in a variety of environments, including woods and deserts.

Tree Kangaroo:

Tree kangaroos are marsupials that have evolved to living in trees and can be found in New Guinea and Australia's rainforests.

For balance, they have powerful limbs and a long, muscular tail.

Tree kangaroos eat leaves and fruits and are herbivores.

These creatures contribute to our planet's extraordinary diversity of life by displaying a variety of adaptations and behaviors.

Did you know!

U

Uakari:

Uakaris are Amazon rainforest monkeys distinguished by their hairless faces and bright red facial skin.

There are various uakaris species, each having differing degrees of reddish on their faces.

Uakaris eat mostly fruits and seeds.

Uguisu Japanese Bush Warbler :

The uguisu, also known as the Japanese bush warbler, is a tiny bird native to Japan, China, and Korea.

It is well-known in Japan for its peculiar and melodic song, which is connected with the onset of spring.

In Japanese poetry and literature, the uguisu has cultural significance.

Urial:

Urial is a Central Asian wild sheep species.

Males have long, curled horns, but females have shorter, straighter horns.

Urials are mountain dwellers who are well adapted to harsh, rocky terrain.

Uinta Ground Squirrel :

Uinta ground squirrels are tiny rodents found in western North America.

They are well-known for their burrowing tendencies and are most active in the summer.

During the winter, Uinta ground squirrels hibernate.

Umbrellafish:

The umbrellafish is a deep-sea fish that is distinguished by its transparent, umbrella-like crest.

These fish, which live in the Atlantic Ocean, use their crest to attract prey by forming a silhouette against the surface.

Umbrellafish have bioluminescent organs that could help them communicate.

Urutu:

The urutu, commonly known as the Bothrops alternatus, is a South American poisonous pit viper.

It is the cause of many snakebites throughout its habitat and is regarded medically significant.

Urutu is mostly active at night and feeds on small mammals, birds, and amphibians.

Despite the fact that the list of animals beginning with "U" is small, each species contributes to the biodiversity of their respective ecosystems.

Umbrellabird:

Umbrellabirds are big black birds that are native to Central and South America.

Males employ an inflatable neck pouch or "umbrella" during courtship displays.

Umbrellabirds play a part in seed dissemination through their feeding patterns.

Umbrellatoothed Tetrarogidae Deep-sea Spider:

The umbrella toothed tetrarogidae are deep-sea spiders that live in the Pacific Ocean.

These spiders have adapted to life in the deep sea, where they trap food with silk and venom.

Despite the fact that the list of animals beginning with "U" is small, each species contributes to the biodiversity of their respective ecosystems.

V

Vulture:

Vultures are scavenging birds of prey that eat dead animals' carcasses.

They have a good sense of sight and can detect carrion from great heights.

Vervet Monkey:

Vervet monkeys are distinguished by their distinctive blue scrotums, which serve as a symbol of dominance.

They are highly gregarious creatures who dwell in groups known as troops.

Vampire Bats:

Vampire bats are the only mammals that consume exclusively blood.

Their noses contain sophisticated heat sensors that detect blood arteries beneath the skin.

Vicuña:

The vicuna is a savage South American camel related to the alpaca.

Vicunas were originally regarded a royal treasure by the Inca civilization due to its exquisite and costly wool.

Vaquita:

The vaquita is a critically endangered porpoise that lives in the Gulf of California.

It is the most endangered cetacean species, with only a few individuals left.

Viperfish:

The viperfish is a deep-sea fish that is distinguished by its long, fang-like teeth and bioluminescent photophores.

They are mainly found in the deep ocean, where they entice prey with their dazzling features.

Velvet Worm:

Velvet worms are ancient invertebrates that live in the tropics and subtropics.

They use a sticky slime to capture their prey, which is a unique hunting tactic.

Vultures Bee:

Vulture bees are bees that feed on decaying flesh and carrion.

They are well-known for their characteristic scavenging on animal carcasses.

Vice Lizard :

The monitor lizard Varanus exanthematicus is sometimes known as the vicelike lizard.

They are recognized for their powerful jaws and sharp teeth, which allow them to consume a wide range of animals.

Vanga Bird:

Vanga birds are located in Madagascar and are distinguished by their distinctive hooked beak.

Vanga birds come in a variety of species, each adapted to a different ecological niche.

These are just a few examples of creatures that begin with the letter "V," demonstrating the animal kingdom's diverse and interesting universe.

W

Whale:

Whales are the world's largest creatures, with some species reaching lengths of more than 100 feet.

The blue whale is the largest mammal known to have ever existed.

Wolf:

Wolves are highly sociable animals that hunt in packs and raise their young together.

The gray wolf is one of the most common and adaptable mammals on the planet.

Walrus:

Walruses are big marine creatures with unique whiskers and powerful tusks.

They use their tusks for a variety of purposes, such as dragging themselves out of water and breaking breathing holes in ice.

Wombat:

Wombats are marsupials native to Australia and its neighboring islands.

They feature a unique backward-facing pouch that keeps soil out during digging.

Woodpecker:

Woodpeckers have particular characteristics that allow them to bore into trees for insects and make various drumming sounds.

They utilize their lengthy tongues to retrieve insects from wood fissures.

Wallaby:

Wallabies are related to kangaroos and are tiny to medium-sized marsupials.

They are herbivores with strong rear legs for jumping.

Warthog:

Warthogs are African wild pigs notable for their characteristic facial warts and tusks.

They are omnivores who dig and root in the dirt with their powerful tusks.

Weasel:

Weasels are small carnivorous mammals with long, slender bodies that are known for their agility as hunters.

They are well-known for their ability to fit into small spaces in order to catch prey.

Wolverine:

Wolverines are carnivores who live in northern latitudes and are noted for their power and perseverance.

Despite their name, they are not related to wolves, but rather to weasels.

White Rhinoceros:

The white rhinoceros is one of the largest rhinoceros species, distinguished by its huge mouth.

Despite its name, the "white" in white rhinoceros is a mistranslation of the Dutch word "wijde," which means "wide" and alludes to its broad mouth.

Whiptail Lizard:

Whiptail lizards are known for their long, slender bodies and tails, which they use for balance.

Some whiptail lizard species are parthenogenetic, which means they can reproduce without fertilization.

Water Buffalo:

Water buffaloes are large herbivores that have been domesticated for a variety of reasons, including agriculture and transportation.

They are well adapted to aquatic environments and often submerged themselves in water to cool off.

These are just a few examples of the diverse range of animals that begin with the letter "W." Each species has distinct characteristics that contribute to the animal kingdom's richness.

Did you know!

X

X-Ray Tetra:

The X-ray tetra is a small, freshwater fish found in the Amazon River basin.

It is named for its translucent body, allowing its internal organs to be partially visible, resembling an X-ray image.

Xantus's Hummingbird:

This species of hummingbird is found in Baja California and is known for its vibrant plumage.

Xantus's hummingbird is named after the Hungarian zoologist John Xantus de Vesey.

Xoloitzcuintli (Mexican Hairless Dog):

The Xoloitzcuintli, often referred to as the Xolo, is a hairless breed of dog that originated in Mexico.

It has a long history, dating back to ancient Aztec times, and is considered a symbol of protection and good luck.

Xenops:

Xenops is a genus of small birds found in Central and South America.

They are known for their distinctive long bills and are part of the woodcreeper family.

X-ray Fusilier:

The X-ray fusilier is a species of tropical fish found in the Indo-Pacific region.

It gets its name from the transparent appearance of its body, similar to an X-ray image.

Y

Yak:

Yaks are large, shaggy-haired mammals found in the Himalayan region.

They are well-adapted to high altitudes and are often domesticated for their milk, meat, and wool.

Yellow-Eyed Penguin:

Also known as Hoiho, the yellow-eyed penguin is native to New Zealand.

It is characterized by distinctive yellow eyes and is one of the rarest penguin species.

Yellow Warbler:

Yellow warblers are small, brightly colored birds found in North and South America.

They are known for their vibrant yellow plumage and melodious songs.

Yellow Baboon:

Yellow baboons are primates native to Africa.

They are social animals, living in groups called troops, and are known for their distinctive yellow fur and dog-like muzzles.

Yellow Tang:

The yellow tang is a brightly colored marine fish found in the Pacific Ocean, particularly around coral reefs.

It is popular in the aquarium trade for its vibrant yellow coloration.

Yellowhead Jawfish:

This species of jawfish is found in the Caribbean Sea and the Gulf of Mexico.

Known for their burrowing behavior, they create and maintain burrows in the sand.

Yabby:

Yabbies are freshwater crustaceans found throughout Australia.

They resemble miniature lobsters and are widely kept in freshwater aquariums.

Yakushima Macaque:

Also known as the Yakushima macaque or the Yakuzaru, these macaques are native to Japan.

They are noted for their cultural value and are often connected with hot springs.

Yellow-Billed Hornbill:

Found in Africa, the yellow-billed hornbill is recognized for its bright yellow beak.

They are cavity nesters, often exploiting tree hollows for nesting.

Yellow-Pine Chipmunk:

Yellow-pine chipmunks are tiny rodents native to western North America.

They are notable for their cheek pouches, which they utilize to carry food.

These are just a few instances of animals whose names begin with the letter "Y."

While the list is not exhaustive due to the small number of animals whose names begin with "Y," each species contributes distinct features to the natural world.

Z

Zebra:

Zebras are noted for their characteristic black-and-white striped coat, which is unique to each individual.

They are gregarious animals that frequently congregate in huge groups to protect themselves from predators.

Zebu:

Zebus are domestic cattle that originated in South Asia.

They are well-adapted to hot regions and are widely utilized in agriculture as draught animals.

Zonkey:

A zonkey is a cross between a donkey and a zebra.

These hybrids frequently exhibit traits from both parents, such as striped legs and a more donkey-like physique.

Zorilla:

The zorilla, sometimes known as the striped polecat, is a tiny carnivorous mammal native to Africa.

It is not connected to actual polecats, despite its name.

Duiker, the zebra:

The zebra duiker is a tiny antelope that can be found in Liberia, Sierra Leone, and the Ivory Coast.

The zebra-like stripes on its back give it its name.

Zebrafish:

Zebrafish are freshwater fish that are native to South Asia.

Because of their translucent embryos, which allow for simple observation of developmental processes, they are extensively utilized in scientific study.

Salamander with a zigzag pattern:

The zigzag salamander is a salamander species native to the southeastern United States.

It gets its name from the zigzag pattern on its back.

Zebra Shark:

The Indo-Pacific region is home to zebra sharks, often known as leopard sharks.

Despite their name, they lack the typical black-and-white stripes of terrestrial zebras and instead feature a spotty pattern.

Zebroid:

A zebroid is a zebra cross with another equine, such as a horse or a pony.

The appearance can vary greatly depending on the specific coupling.

Zander:

The zander is a freshwaterr fish that is native to Europe and Western Asia.

It is a popular recreational fishing spot.

Zorse:

A zorse is an animal that is a cross between a zebra and a horse.

A zorse's appearance can vary, with some individuals having a blend of stripes and solid-colored fur.

Zokor:

Zokors are burrowing rodents from Asia.

They have a sturdy, cylindrical body and are well-suited to a subterranean existence.

Conclusion

We have studied the magnificent tapestry of the animal kingdom in the engaging trip through "Facts About Animals," revealing a world brimming with diversity, wonder, and astounding truths. The book has exposed the amazing intricacies that make each species unique, from the nuanced activities of the tiniest insects to the majestic capabilities of apex predators. The overwhelming message as we conclude the pages is clear: the natural world is a marvel of evolution, and our fellow dwellers on this planet are both awe-inspiring and essential to the delicate balance of existence. "Facts About Animals" is a celebration of nature's fascinating stories, urging readers to marvel at the grandeur and complexities of the wild areas that surround us.

Did you know!

www.ingramcontent.com/pod-product-compliance
Lightning Source LLC
Chambersburg PA
CBHW070931260726
48661CB00003B/939